the
Book
that
reads
me

Hans-Ruedi Weber

the Book
that reads me

A Handbook **for Bible Study Enablers**

Published for the World Student Christian Federation
by WCC Publications, Geneva

Cover design: Edwin Hassink

Cover photo: Michael Dominguez

Cover illustration: Wood sculpture by an unknown Tanzanian artist

ISBN 2-8254-1164-7

© 1995 WCC Publications, World Council of Churches,
150 route de Ferney, 1211 Geneva 2, Switzerland

Printed in Switzerland

Contents

Preface

This guide was originally prepared for a Bible study enablers' training course, organized jointly by the World Student Christian Federation and the Ecumenical Institute of the World Council of Churches in Bossey, Switzerland (February-March 1995).

Nearly fifteen years have passed since my handbook *Experiments with Bible Study* (Geneva, WCC, 1981) was published. This book has been widely used, reprinted several times and translated in a number of other languages. In its English version it is now out of print. While some shortened paragraphs from this earlier publication appear in what follows, this guide also sums up new insights I have gained in biblical teaching since the early 1980s.

H-RW

Introduction

The Bible: a book?

"Yes, a book." So most people would answer. But is this really true? If we are thinking in terms of books, it would be more precise to say that the Bible is a whole library. From a purely literary point of view, it is a library composed of 66 volumes — and even more if one follows the listing of the Septuagint, the Greek translation of the Hebrew scriptures. The books in this library were written over a period from about 1000 years before Christ to about 100 years after his birth. Some of these "volumes" are mere two-page letters, like the one to Philemon; others are much more substantial epistles, stories and testimonies. Several are complicated literary documents in which an editor has put together different sources, accounts and interpretations of the same series of events. This is the case, for instance, with the books of Genesis and Exodus. The four gospels were such a new type of literature that for a long time people did not know what to call them. Finally, there are volumes in this library, like the book of Psalms or the books of Isaiah and Jeremiah, which consist of small, separate libraries in themselves.

But if we see the Bible in the first place as a book, as a collection of literary documents, we do not really do justice to how the biblical traditions of faith have functioned in the course of history. How did the masses of people have access to the biblical messages before book printing was invented in the fifteenth century? For although biblical manuscripts existed in the centuries before that, they were rare and costly. Moreover, a large percentage of church members could not read. The Bible as a manuscript or a book remained a treasure inaccessible to them. Yet they also did "Bible study", though in ways which we may not immediately recognize as such, because for most of us both the terms "Bible" and "study" have almost exclusively literary connotations.

This guide will describe some of the ways in which the biblical faith traditions were transmitted, learned, appropriated and studied in the course of history. We will see that already in biblical times such a variety of methods was used. These various ways of learning can still teach us a great deal. In the "Suggestions for Bible Study", printed at the end of each chapter, indications are given of how groups can explore the biblical messages in both literary and non-literary ways.

The secret of Bible study

The small wood sculpture by an unknown Tanzanian artist which is reproduced on the cover of this book stands on my desk. As one looks at the tattooed face of this African woman, it seems that a big smile is just beginning to break through. Is she going to reveal a great secret which gives her deep joy?

The artist has captured the climax of a story told in East Africa. A village woman used to walk around always carrying her Bible. "Why always the Bible?" her neighbours asked teasingly. "There are so many other books you could read." The woman knelt down, held the Bible high above her head and said, "Yes, of course there are many books which I could read. But there is only one book which reads me."

This African woman perceived the mystery of Bible study. We can listen to biblical stories, read and study the biblical texts or look at great art based on biblical events and themes simply as works of human experience and inspiration. We should indeed do so in order fully to appreciate the poetry, the art of story-telling and the wisdom found in the biblical literature and its imagery. The library now called the Bible is shaped by human witnesses, communicates through human languages and has been marked by the cultures of the ancient Near East and the Roman empire. This human dimension of the Bible must never be disregarded, just as it would be wrong to ignore the human nature of Jesus of Nazareth. Otherwise the Bible becomes an idol which we worship and the incarnation of Jesus is denied.

However, as we listen, read, study and try to see, a reversal of roles can take place. We start out being the subjects. The biblical messages, in whatever form they reach us, are the objects of our study. Then suddenly we may become aware that behind and through the stories, texts and visualized messages stands someone who looks at us, speaks to us and gives us guidance. The object of our enquiry becomes the subject who addresses us and understands us better than we do ourselves. We are confronted with the living God who acts in creation and history, in our personal life and in the world of nations. In Bible study we may experience already now something of what the apostle Paul once wrote to the Christians in Corinth: "Now we see in a mirror, dimly, but then we will see face to face. Now I know only in part; then I will know fully, even as I have been fully known."

Some comments about methods

This mysterious reversal of roles cannot be triggered by methods. It comes by the power of the Holy Spirit, the communicator and interpreter. We can and must pray that the mystery of Bible study may happen. "Come, Creator Spirit!" And while we do so, we must use the best methods for letting biblical stories, texts and images speak to us. Therefore we have much to learn from the various ways in which the biblical witnesses themselves transmitted the messages they received and how they imprinted them on the memories and hearts of those whom they addressed.

The term "method" (from the Greek *methodos, methodeia*) points to something very significant for the process of communication. Literally, it means to follow a way (in Greek, *hodos*) together with others. However, in the New Testament this term occurs only twice and both times in a pejorative sense, referring to the devil who has *methodeia*, that is, "clever devices" and a "craftiness" to lead people astray (Eph. 4:14,

6:11). This is a necessary warning for those who want to learn Bible study methods. Methods can be of the devil. With methods one can manipulate people and distort the very messages one wants to communicate.

However, nobody should ignore methods. Those who do so are unconsciously using only one method — and not necessarily the best one. They may resort simply to lecturing, which runs the risk of making the audience completely passive. It is possible to transform such one-way teaching into a common search for truth in which each one participates. Methods are thus very important, because they can become either channels for or obstacles to the Holy Spirit. For the same reason methods are very unimportant, because only the Spirit has the power to cause a process of communication to succeed. In any case, thorough preparation is needed with regard to both content and method, and no one should mistakenly assume that methods which foster group participation need less preparation than lectures.

No ideal Bible study method exists. For each biblical passage, theme or image the most appropriate way must be discerned. Much depends on the group with which one works: the number of participants, their special interests, their motivations. One must also examine which methods can or cannot be used in the time and meeting place which are available for the study. Sometimes one is unable to use a very "successful" or fascinating method because it would overshadow or even betray the biblical messages which the biblical authors want to convey.

Worksheets for study

Often it is good to prepare and distribute a worksheet to the participants in a group Bible study. For instance, such a one- or two-page paper can show different translations of the chosen biblical passage if this helps the study. For a passage from a gospel, one may want to reproduce a synopsis, highlighting the dfferences in how that story is recorded in two or more gospels by placing the accounts side by side. Sometimes it is helpful to print together with the biblical passage a text from the Jewish or Hellenistic world in which it was originally told or written. A photocopy of an ancient or modern art work, of a map or photographs of a relevant archaeological discovery can stimulate group discussion.

The worksheet may also include two or three questions to help both the study of the biblical passage and the discovery of its messages for today. Phrasing the right questions is the most difficult part of animating participatory Bible study. Often the best question will be found — by the animator or by a group member — only during the process of group study itself. Worksheets must therefore remain open-ended, allowing for ways of exploration which the enabler did not foresee during the preparation.

The use of additional material always runs the risk that participants will discuss the worksheet instead of the biblical testimonies. What is true for the methods is true also for the media with which one works. Worksheets, cassettes, drawings, slides, videos and the like have to serve Bible study. They must not draw attention away from the messages which the biblical witnesses intended to convey.

Bible studies with large groups

Participatory Bible study can best be done in a group of seven to fifteen people and an animator/enabler who proceeds in a Socratic way: through questions stimulating a common search. But even in a much larger group this Socratic approach and the active participation of all need not be abandoned. One does not always have to fall back on the lecture method.

In almost all seating arrangements it is possible for participants to talk with one or two neighbours sitting beside them (sometimes called "buzz-groups"). After some introductory remarks the animator poses a question about the biblical story, text, image or theme to be studied and asks all participants to reflect individually about it for two or three minutes. These moments of silent reflection are essential because in every group there are quick and slow thinkers, and the former are not necessarily the deep thinkers. The question is then talked over with one's immediate neighbours. This enables timid participants to contribute and gives talkative ones a chance to "let off steam". After giving some opportunity for feedback from participants, the animator proceeds with further comments and a new question.

If the hall is too large for direct feedback, two or three representative participants can be asked to sit together with the animator on the platform and act as a panel. After the whole assembly has reflected on and discussed a given question with their neighbours for a few minutes, this panel enters into a spontaneous public discussion with the animator. In this way participatory Bible study can be animated with a group of several hundred, even with a few thousand participants.

The group and the animator/enabler

Since this guide deals with group study and not with mass communication, it does not discuss such methods and media as lecturing through microphones to large crowds, radio and television programmes and films. For participatory group work direct eye contact is necessary, and it is ideal if the group can sit together in a circle with the animator.

Paul reminds us that each one has something to contribute (1 Cor. 14:26). It may simply be what is sometimes called "a stupid question", which will often in fact prove to be a genuine stimulus to further thinking. The contribution may also be a sudden insight, a word of wisdom, a critical comment or the frank expression of doubts. The presence in the group of seekers and persons from outside Christian circles usually helps overly pious Christians honestly to face questions of truth. Whenever an animator thinks that he or she knows it all and does not trust that all participants have received gifts and insights, Bible study becomes stale.

Timid or slow group members must have a chance to contribute and members who are too talkative must be held back. To ensure this, the procedure of "buzz-groups" described above for large groups can also be used in a small circle: after introductory remarks, ask a question, give time for individual reflection, then time for discussion with one's neighbours, followed by general discussion leading to further teaching and questions.

The animator has the double task of watching that the biblical messages remain in the centre of attention and that all participants can join in the common search. Enablers are therefore the advocates of both the Bible and the quiet and hesitant members of the group. Only in this way can corporate Bible study become and remain a voyage of discovery. It may not degenerate into a sharing of ignorance or a repetition of the theological "hobby horses" of either the participants or the animator. When a Bible study tells us only what we already know or simply confirms our often biased beliefs, it may be an indication that we are approaching the Bible like a ventriloquist, hearing only what we in fact want to *say*, rather than letting God speak to us.

While emphasizing the participation of all, the animator must not neglect the actual teaching. Often a short lecture input is therefore needed. Such straightforward teaching can best be done — after thorough preparation — by the animator or a group member rather than by an "expert" from outside who does not participate in the whole study process.

Bible study enablers must know their own special gifts and limitations. Not everyone can use all methods proposed. However, the gifts of grace, the *charismata*, are not static entities. Gifts received but not used decay. Through prayer and hard work new gifts can be acquired. Often it takes courage to try a new method, but it is only in doing that one learns.

The suggestions for Bible study

Each of the following chapters ends with a series of suggestions for actual group Bible studies. All of these have been tested in practice. Often two or three different methods were used in the same study session. Not all these studies always went well. However, it is my experience that sometimes both the group and the animator learn most when a study session does not proceed smoothly or is even experienced as a "failure". The fact that many central questions remained unanswered can become a stimulus for better preparation. The feeling that one was not up to the challenge of what the biblical witnesses wanted to convey leads to continuing prayer and search. The awareness that the study did not really speak to the participants helps us to become more sensitive to the questions of our own time.

Those who use this guide and try to animate Bible studies according to these suggestions should not follow them slavishly. The suggestions are not fixed models but are intended to stimulate the user's own search for the best ways to help groups discover that unique book *which reads us.*

I

The Bible as Oral Tradition

From mouth to ear

Hearing has primacy in the Bible over reading and seeing. "Hear, Israel" is the beginning of the instruction which each believing Jew recites daily (Deut. 6:4). The great majority of testimonies contained in the Bible were communicated orally long before they became fixed in writing. The Torah was not a book of divine laws but the will and the instructions of the living God, addressed from mouth to ear. Even after the later priests and scribes had written it on scrolls, it still had to be proclaimed aloud to the people. In 622 B.C. King Josiah "read in their hearing all the words of the book of the covenant" (2 Kings 23:2). Some two centuries later the priest-scribe Ezra did the same (Neh. 8:1-8).

This inherent emphasis on hearing in the biblical testimonies is not in the first place due to widespread illiteracy. The literate rabbis of Jesus' time also did not write books; rather, they instructed by discussing with one another and with their disciples. Only around the end of the second century after Christ was their oral teaching from mouth to ear fixed in writing in the Mishnah and other collections.

Jesus was such an oral teacher, and he used the whole register of the oral tradition: stories, parables, proverbs, rhythmic language, gestures and tangible tokens. Detailed studies have shown how the flavour of the oral Aramaic teaching of Jesus can still be detected in the Greek text of the gospels. In the early church the literary documents of the letters of Paul and the text of the gospels were carefully copied and transmitted, but the oral testimony maintained priority over the written text. Even after all the parts which later formed the

New Testament had been fixed in writing, Papias, the bishop of Hierapolis, wrote in the early second century that he trusted the living testimony of witnesses more than what one could get from books. There is wisdom in this. The faith traditions need to be reaccentuated ever again for new hearers. Biblical messages have to pass through a living witness, a living voice. The second Helvetic Confession of 1566 put it boldly: "The preaching of the word of God *is* the word of God." Oral communication can of course be done in a much more participatory way than through preaching. Yet even in preaching the two major advantages of the oral tradition which we have mentioned become obvious: the presence of a personal witness and the freedom to reinterpret a received message for ever new persons and situations.

The training of the memory

Both in biblical times and in later church history the inherent dangers of oral transmission became evident. That which gives communication from mouth to ear its richness is also its weakness: the messages to be communicated are gradually changed. Important elements may be lost through human forgetfulness. Other parts will be unduly expanded through human inventiveness. It was therefore essential for the oral biblical testimonies to be fixed in writing and for the Bible also to become a literary document (see chapter II).

The presence of manuscripts did not mean that the process of oral communication stopped. During the early Christian centuries there was already a considerable amount of individual Bible reading. However, reading in antiquity meant reading aloud: from the text to the eye and by way of the mouth to the ear. The evangelist Philip heard the Ethiopian eunuch reading the scroll of Isaiah (Acts 8:28,30). Such reading and recitation aloud was used for memorization, not simply for learning by rote but for an inner appropriation of the message, for the translation of the text from writing into the heart. A little-known New Testament beatitude says: "Blessed is the one who reads aloud the words of the prophecy, and blessed are those who hear and who keep what is written in it" (Rev. 1:3). Manuscripts functioned as an *aide-mémoire*: they were helps for remembering, for checking the remembered message, for reflecting on it and interiorizing it. The messages received could thus be learned, celebrated in worship, taught and proclaimed to others.

In synagogue schools the pupils learned not simply how to read but, more importantly, how to memorize. They were instructed in various techniques, for instance how to use rhythmic body movements for memorization. They learned how the first word and the key term of a biblical passage or book are important for remembering. Jews in fact designate the books of the Hebrew scriptures by the first word of their first sentence: thus the book of Genesis is called *bereshîth*, "In the beginning". Pupils also learned to recognize and use link-passages for remembering and reciting a whole series of stories or instructions in the right sequence.

At that time people were still aware of an insight which Plato attributes to Socrates, who told the story of the Egyptian god Teuth, who boasted of having invented the letters, claiming that he had found "an elixir of memory and wisdom". Teuth's claim was rightly rejected:

> Your invention will produce forgetfulness in the minds of those who learn to use it, because they will not practise their memory... You have invented an elixir not of memory but of reminding; and you offer your pupils the appearance of wisdom, not true wisdom, for they will read many things without instruction and will therefore seem to know many things, when they are for the most part ignorant (*Phaedrus*, 274f.).

In a time when the printed Bible is so easily available that memorization seems unnecessary, and when computers have such powerful memories, this wise warning takes on new importance. As we leave our living memories untrained and at the same time receive so much undigested information every day, the shallow appearance of "knowledge" increases. At the same time, biblical illiteracy is becoming more widespread.

Rediscovering the Bible as oral tradition is a good antidote to this modern loss of memory and shallowness of knowledge. Study which includes all three — hearing, memorizing and telling — can become true meditation: the message heard is being translated into the heart. Biblical testimonies then become part of our frame of reference. They inform our understanding and shape our lives.

Telling the story

The great biblical stories have been transmitted so that they can be told. For telling a story eye-to-eye contact is needed, not eyes fixed on the notes. The story must be learned by heart. This does not mean that the exact wording of the written story needs to be slavishly memorized. But the key terms that have been discerned, the right sequence of the sub-scenes and the significant movements and pronouncements of the actors in the story have to be well remembered and told. A good narration thus demands both a considerable degree of understanding of the meaning of the story and of memorization.

Narrators must enter emotionally into the story and grasp its plot, so that while telling it they inwardly see what is happening. This participation in the story will shape the right timbre and appropriate loudness or quietness of the voice. It will dictate the moments of speed, slowness or silence in the course of story-telling and also help to find the right look in the eye and the right gestures. All these non-literary aspects of communication are absent if the text is read silently. In story-telling they are as essential as what is actually said.

Many biblical stories are "counter-stories", in which things happen or are said which hearers would not naturally expect. Often there are sudden twists, reversals and amazing conclusions, as in most parables of Jesus. For good story-telling it is important to be sensitive to anything that does not fit the expected pattern. Often it is exactly at those surprising turns that the true meaning of the story appears.

Story-telling should if possible involve the hearers. Yet those addressed must be allowed the freedom either to remain simply active listeners or to become participants in the story-telling through interjections, comments, questions or even protest. If the story is well told, listeners will soon discover the challenging relationship between the old biblical story and their own present-day life story. No interpretation or actualization is then needed; indeed, concluding "theological reflections" may risk destroying the impact of the story and its own inherent narrative theology.

Recently, examples of "narrative exegesis" have been orally presented and later published. In biblical commentaries historical, social, economic and religious background information is usually given in introductions or in footnotes. Narrative exegesis incorporates such helpful information for understanding into the story itself. Similarly, instead of making exegetical comments about how the meaning of a story has been differently understood, narrative exegesis displays such varying interpretations through the dialogues and attitudes of the actors in the story.

Singing the message

In all cultures oral tradition and singing have been intimately linked. The Bible too contains many passages which were originally sung. This applies first of all to most of the Psalms and to the hymns, such as the ancient songs of Miriam and Deborah (Ex. 15:21; Judg. 5), the canticles in Luke 1 and 2 and the early Christian hymns quoted in several New Testament letters and the book of Revelation. But non-poetic passages were also originally not only recited but chanted. Ancient Hebrew manuscripts contain signs which are almost certainly musical annotations. Attempts have been made to decipher these signs or to go back from ancient Jewish singing to the original biblical melodies.

The therapeutic influence of music was known in biblical times (1 Sam. 16:14ff.), and music played a role in prophecy (1 Sam. 10:5f.). Singing was prominent in worship, both in family celebrations and especially in the temple of Jerusalem. The Chronicler writes about the 288 trained singers and

120 trumpeters of the temple (1 Chron. 25:7; 2 Chron. 5:12). Jesus maintained the Jewish custom of singing Psalms (Mark 14:26), and Paul exhorted the Christians: "With gratitude in your hearts sing Psalms, hymns and spiritual songs to God" (Col. 3:16). One of the earliest extra-biblical accounts of worship in the ancient church — from Pliny in the early second century — says that Christians "were in the habit of meeting on a certain fixed day before it was light, when they sang in alternative verses a hymn to Christ, as a god".

Throughout the centuries the singing of Psalms and hymns remained the most common way to praise God and the best way to imprint biblical passages and messages on the mind and heart. Until the ninth century, Christian hymns were sung in unison. Thereafter rich polyphonic melodies, with instrumental accompaniment, were developed. Important stages in this development were Byzantine liturgical music, mediaeval Western monastic psalmody and anthems, the Psalms and hymns of the Reformation and the classical oratorios. In many evangelistic renewal movements — for example, Methodism — singing the biblical faith became central. More recently the African-American spirituals, folk masses in Latin America and Africa, modern symphonic cantatas and a plethora of new biblical hymns and sung liturgical responses have become widely known carriers of biblical oral tradition.

Suggestions for Bible Studies
Based on Oral Tradition

Reading aloud

No Bible study should be made without hearing the biblical passage to be examined. If the text is not too long, the animator can ask two or three participants before the meeting of the group to learn to read the assigned passage well. The study then begins with two or three readings of the same text.

A study of 2 Samuel 12:1-7a or of Mark 14:3-9 may thus proceed in the following way. After listening to several readings of the passage, the group discusses critically the various ways of reading. This will lead to such questions as: How did the voice of the prophet Nathan change from 2 Samuel 12:1b-4 to 12:7a? What function does the parable have in this passage? With what intonation must the words of Mark 14:4b-5a and of Mark 14:6-9 be read? What does Jesus' response teach us about his ministry and destiny?

These two passages, like many others in the Bible, can also be read dramatically, using one reader for the text which is not in direct speech and different voices for each of the actors in the story. Often it is helpful to record such a reading on a cassette with divided roles and then to play it back. We hear differently if we are directly involved in reading from the way we hear when we listen to a recorded reading.

One of the most moving ways of doing Bible study during Passion Week is to prepare together as a group and then record a dramatic reading, with divided voices, of Mark 11:1-11, 14:1-15:41. To have to cry as a member of the crowd first "Hosanna!" and then "Crucify him!" will help many people to enter into the drama of passion more than many sermons.

Learning to memorize and tell

A good way of doing Bible study is simply to learn a biblical narrative by heart and then tell it to others. Stories from the Acts and the gospels and narrative passages in the Old Testament lend themselves best to this exercise.

For those who are new to story-telling the following preparatory exercise is helpful. Each participant chooses a partner. The two tell one another a favourite joke, with the listener carefully observing the teller. Then they discuss what they have learned about good or bad story-telling. If time permits, this reflection about story-telling can lead to a general discussion.

For memorization, the following procedure, also using teams of two, has proved effective:

The chosen biblical story is read aloud by one partner while the other listens without following in the printed text. Then the roles are reversed. The listener becomes the reader.

After this initial reading and hearing, the two partners decide together how to divide the story into several sub-scenes. Each episode of the story is given a title, using the key terms of that episode. The sequence of titles is then well memorized.

Now one partner tells the story from memory while the other checks in the text to see if important parts have been left out or new things added. This is repeated with the one who checked becoming the narrator and vice-versa. The two help one another to find the right intonation, speed and, if needed, one or two gestures while telling (but beware of too much gesticulation).

After about 20 to 30 minutes, most participants will know how to tell the story from memory if they have concentrated during these exercises on the task of memorizing and telling and not spent their time talking about the story.

The whole group then assembles, and volunteers are asked to tell the story to the others. At that time some discussion about the story, its meaning and message may be needed. Usually, however, the story, which has been told and heard several times, has already made its point.

Counter-stories

Many biblical stories and events have sudden unexpected twists and astonishing reversals. Since they do not proceed as one might expect, they are in fact "counter-stories", challenging human thinking and reasoning. With many events in the Bible, it is only when listening to a version of the story as one would have expected it to proceed that one fully discovers its newness and challenging nature. This can be illustrated by Jesus' meeting with Zacchaeus (Luke 19:1-10).

Participants are asked not to open their Bibles. The animator or a group member then tells a previously memorized "revised version" of the Zacchaeus story, following the account as told by Luke but changing it at a crucial point to conform to the way one might have expected it to happen. Would not Jesus, the friend of the poor, have defended the poor against the wealthy Zacchaeus who was exploiting them? Would he not have judged him and told him what he told the rich young ruler (Luke 18:22f.)? And would Zacchaeus, hearing this, not have gone home sadly, like the rich ruler?

Having listened to this new version of the story, the participants are asked to debate with one another whether they believe this new account could also stand in the gospels. After all, many stories about Jesus are told differently in the different gospels. Is the Jesus of the alternative version the Jesus whom we know from the gospels? In this debate the animator should not take sides, at most supporting minority voices if needed.

Keeping their Bibles closed, group members are then asked to reconstruct from their memory the biblical version of the story as Luke told it. This can best be done in buzz-groups. Several of those reconstructed biblical versions are then told to the whole group.

Only after this oral work are Bibles opened and the biblical text read. Participants will by then be eager to read the story as Luke recorded it. This leads to the question: What can we learn about Jesus from Luke's version of this story? In what way is Luke's version a counter-story, challenging and correcting our stereotypes of what Jesus' ministry is?

A narrative exegesis

Preparing and telling a narrative exegesis requires considerable background knowledge and exegetical insight. The following exercise, based on Acts 17:1-9, requires two sessions and homework in between.

In a first session the group examines the account of Paul's visit to Thessalonica in the year 50 and the uproar which happened there. This is done in a historical-literary way, with participants being given information about the growing emperor worship, the political and economic situation of the city of Thessalonica in the Roman empire and the nascent tensions between Jews and Christians at that time. Examining the text will show the difference between what Paul actually taught in the synagogue and what he is accused of having said.

At the end of the first session, participants are asked to prepare a narrative exegesis on this passage for the next session. They should assume that in the winter of 50-51, the Roman procunsul of Thessalonica was ordered by the emperor Claudius to report about what happened in that strategically located city when Paul was there. The proconsul therefore questions Jason, representatives of the Jewish synagogue, the city authorities and members of the mob. What did he hear? What did he ultimately report to Claudius?

During the second session, members of the group tell their stories. This exercise will help participants to understand the power politics behind many biblical passages as well as the precarious situation of the early church and its mission in the Roman empire.

A song for the Lord

Bible study receives a new tonality and greater participation if it is related to singing. Here are five examples of how this might be done.

Begin the group study of a Psalm — for example, Psalm 100 — by singing one of the traditional musical settings of it. Then examine the probable original setting of the Psalm chosen, the imagery of its language and its main messages. On this basis, the group members look critically at the text and melody of the traditional musical version of the Psalm. Is it faithful to the poetry, spirituality and messages of the original biblical text? Does the traditional melody still communicate for present-day sensibilities what the author of the Psalm wanted to communicate? What "corrections" in melody and text of the traditionally sung Psalm would be needed in order to communicate the feelings and messages of the original biblical Psalm today? Participants might then try to rewrite the Psalm using contemporary imagery and a popular current melody without betraying the Psalm's original intention and message.

Listen as a group to recordings of how the Magnificat of Mary (Luke 1:46-55) is traditionally chanted and how it has been rephrased and is sung in a modern song. Learn to chant and sing the Magnificat in these two versions. Then let the group discuss the strengths and weaknesses of each of the two versions. Where do the melody and the words communicate well the intent of Mary's song? Where is this intent weakened, alienated or betrayed?

Study first with the whole group the text and context of one of the short early Christian hymns quoted in the New Testament letters, such as the baptismal hymn in Ephesians 5:14. Then let sub-groups find an appropriate melody for this hymn. The key terms and the message of the text must be maintained, but it may be necessary to change some of the phrasing for rhythmic singing. When the group reassembles, the different new musical versions of the hymn are sung.

Non-poetic texts can also be transformed into biblical songs. In a West African Bible seminar a synoptic study was made of the parable of the sheep that had gone astray (see chapter II, p.21). Participants were then asked to compose a song with a rhythmic melody and drum. The first verse should simply tell the parable, the second and third verses should communicate what we had learned from Luke's and Matthew's version of the parable and the last verse should translate the parable for West Africa. Within a week, that song travelled spontaneously from village to village and was sung by many who had not attended the course.

Ask the group first to compare the hymnic parts of the worship in heaven described in Revelation 4 and 5 with traditional and modern sung responses in eucharistic liturgies. Also study the laments heard on earth while the scroll with seven seals is being opened (Rev. 6:10,16). The group should then try to prepare a script for a worship based on John's vision, with readings, gestures and sung responses and complaints. Even if the script and the sung parts are not perfect, it will be good actually to celebrate this worship, in which there is much movement. For example, for chapters 4 and 5 one might want to go up to an "upper room" and for chapter 6 come down to the earthly scene. No one who has helped to prepare and then participated in such a worship will ever forget this vision of the seer John.

II

The Bible as a Literary Document

From mouth to canonical manuscripts

A few parts of the Bible have from their origin been literary documents. Instances are the edict of Cyrus in 538 B.C., quoted in Ezra 6:3-5, and the letters of the apostle Paul, which were sent to local churches to be read aloud in the congregations (cf. Col. 4:16). Gradually, many of the orally transmitted biblical traditions were also fixed in writing. The process of selecting and ordering the normative Hebrew scriptures probably began already in the time of Ezra (early fourth century B.C.), and it was completed only about A.D. 70, fixing the authoritative guiding list (the "canon") of the Hebrew scriptures, called the *Masora*.

Meanwhile the Jewish scribes in Egypt had translated many of the Hebrew scriptures into Greek. This translation, called the Septuagint, was almost complete towards the end of the second century B.C. Its list of normative scriptures is larger than that of the *Masora*. It includes such so-called deuterocanonical books of the second and first centuries B.C. as Sirach, Baruch, 1 and 2, Maccabees and the Wisdom of Solomon. The Septuagint also has a different ordering of the scriptures from the *Masora*, distinguishing historical, prophetic and poetic writings. Moreover, there is a spiritualizing tendency in this Greek translation, lacking the more earthy quality of the Hebrew scriptures.

In the time of Jesus the Jewish scriptures had become a set of *biblia*, in the form either of separate scrolls or of volumes. Yet there still was considerable discussion and disagreement about which of these *biblia* were the fully authoritative scriptures. Texts from the Torah as well as from the prophets were read, paraphrased and commented on in the synagogue worship (Luke 4:16-22). The Bible of the early church was what we call the Old Testament (many prefer to call it the First Testament): and Christians used both the Hebrew and the Greek versions of the Jewish scriptures.

The canon of the New Testament became more or less fixed only towards the end of the second century after Christ, when the list of the "Muratorian Canon" found acceptance in many circles. Yet both the full list and the ordering of authoritative New Testament writings remained uncertain. The early church thus lived for more than three centuries with an "unfinished" Bible and an open canon. For most of the Eastern churches the list in a letter of Athanasius in A.D. 367 found general acceptance. In the Western church the councils of Hippo (393) and Carthage (397) settled the question of the canon.

Ancient Jewish text studies

Like the priests and scribes of Old Testament times, the Jewish rabbis of Jesus' day continued to copy the biblical text and interpret it orally. Beginning in 1947, parts of the library of the Qumran community were discovered. This Jewish community lived in the Judaean desert from the middle of the second century B.C. to A.D. 70. Among the manuscripts found in this library were not only copies of Old Testament books but also written commentaries on them. Linked with most Jewish synagogues was a *bet-ha-midrash*, a "house of seeking/learning", for rabbinical Bible study and biblical teaching. Moreover, after the destruction of Jerusalem in A.D. 70, rabbinical schools in Palestine, Egypt and especially in Babylonia became centres of Jewish exegesis and biblical scholarship.

Different methods of Jewish text study can be distinguished. The Qumranites reinterpreted the Hebrew scriptures in the light of their own community and especially in the light of the ministry and destiny of their founder, the "teacher of righteousness". The rabbis in Palestine and Babylonia often worked with an interpretation by "resonance": one word or event in a text evoked and recalled the same word or a similar event in many other texts. This led to the discovery of new meanings. A text has to be turned around again and again, they said, so that new facets of meaning appear. The rabbis discussed especially the adaptation and application of old prescriptions of the Torah to their own time and they searched for the biblical basis of new prescriptions and prohibitions for Jewish life (the *halacha*). They also applied the old biblical stories to their own everyday life by using paraphrases and narrative interpretation (the *haggada*). In Hellenistic Judaism the typological method was often used: a person or event in the Hebrew scriptures was seen as a "type", foreshadowing persons and events of later times. Especially in Alexandria, Hellenistic Jewish exegetes also loved to work with allegory: each detail of the biblical text was understood not only in a literal sense but as pointing to deeper layers of meaning.

Early Christian text studies

Paul and other New Testament witnesses used methods of textual interpretation similar to the Jewish ones. However, they did so in the light of the ministry, death and resurrection of Jesus. The New Testament rereading of the Old Testament thus had many similarities to the Qumranite type of exegesis. Typology and allegories played an important role in the Alexandrian school of Christian biblical interpretation, for instance in the commentaries of Origen, which deeply influenced mediaeval Western exegesis. Representatives of the Antiochian school, for instance Theodore the Exegete, rejected allegory, used typology carefully and based their interpretation mainly on the methods of Greek grammatical and historical text studies. Among the Latin church fathers Jerome became the great interpreter and translator of the Bible, summing up for the Western church the insights of the Antiochian and especially the Alexandrian school.

Book printing, original texts and translations

The first book printed in the Western world, just after 1450, was Johannes Gutenberg's 42-line Latin Bible. Already in 1488 a printed Hebrew Bible appeared in northern Italy. The Greek text of the New Testament was printed for the first time in Basel, in 1516, prepared for publication by the humanist Erasmus of Rotterdam. Only a few years later the six volumes of the Complutensian Polyglot Bible were published in Alcala, Spain: in it the Greek, Latin and Hebrew texts with Aramaic paraphrases of the Bible are printed side by side. Completing this great publishing venture were several helps for literary study, such as dictionaries, a biblical grammar and indexes.

The availability of the original text led to many Bible translations which could now be more widely distributed through print. In 1521-22 Martin Luther's New Testament in German became the first success story of book printing. Soon followed translations and printed editions of the whole Bible: the German *Luther-Bibel* in 1534, the English Coverdale Bible in 1535 and the French *Bible d'Olivétan* in 1535.

In the course of the next centuries many tools for the literary text study became available: biblical wordbooks, concordances, atlases, encyclopaedias with archaeological, historical and cultural background information about biblical times, a synopsis of the gospels, biblical word statistics and so on. This led to the publication of numerous new introductions to the Bible and above all to many biblical commentaries. The invention of book-printing in the Renaissance, the humanist's longing to go back to the sources and the search for truth in the time of the Reformation and Counter-Reformation made a deep impact on Bible study. It must be remembered, however, that through the eighteenth century both the production of paper and printing were done manually, so that printed Bibles remained expensive. Only when machines for paper-making and mechanical printing machines were invented in 1803-1804 could the Bible as a book be inexpensively produced and widely distributed.

It is no wonder that at the very same time, in 1804, the first large Bible society was founded. In Roman Catholic and especially in Protestant missionary work, printing and established Western-type schools had a high priority. Soon it was not only in Western society but also in the mainly oral cultures of Africa and the Pacific that the Bible came to be seen in the first place as a book. In order to become a Christian it was almost obligatory to learn to read.

Modern historical-literary approaches to Bible study

The theological confrontations at the time of the Reformation led to intensive studies of the biblical text, which continued during the confessional debates of the seventeenth and eighteenth centuries. In the movements of pietism and spiritual revival Bible study was done mainly for the upbuilding of faith. On a more academic level, biblical exegesis often served polemically to refute heresies or to uncover what were considered to be incorrect dogmatic presuppositions in the position of one's opponent.

This gradually led in the nineteenth and twentieth centuries to the modern historical-literary critical approach in much of Protestant and Roman Catholic and some Orthodox biblical research. A great deal of work, based on the discovery of many ancient biblical manuscripts and even older fragments of biblical papyri, was done to reconstruct as faithfully as possible the original Hebrew and Greek text. Biblical texts were compared with other religious literary documents of Old and New Testament times. Archaeological discoveries shed new light on many biblical passages. Different sources and literary genres were distinguished in the Pentateuch (Genesis to Deuteronomy) and in other parts of the biblical literature. Attention focussed on the question of historicity of the events reported as well as on how the oral tradition was fixed in writing. More recently, historical and text-critical work have concentrated on the authors and first addressees of the biblical writings, on the social and political background of these texts and on the various theologies which characterize them. New forms of literary-linguistic analysis are also being used which do not emphasize the original historical context but read the biblical texts as they speak to us now, analyzing their structure and rhetorical quality and examining the meaning to which these point.

All such modern critical historical-literary methods can help to let the biblical texts speak to us in their own right. Texts which may have become too familiar to many believers suddenly display again their strangeness, giving them new cutting edges. Passages which have been used — and often misused — as prooftexts for this or that dogmatic statement or moral standard are rediscovered in their original context and begin to address us in a new way.

Unfortunately, such critical methods have often functioned mainly in a negative way, challenging and even destroying received faith. And contrary to what is often claimed, these methods of study do not produce a totally "objective" reading of the Bible. They are strongly marked by the presuppositions of the Western literary culture and often measure the biblical testimonies with criteria which are not congenial to the biblical texts. Nevertheless, if used in a pastoral-critical way, such modern historical-literary methods of study help to question bibliolatry, the "worship of the Book", and false conceptions about the authority of the Bible. By testing a faith which is not really based on the biblical witness, they can help to build up a true biblical faith.

Suggestions for Historical-Literary Bible Studies

From print to manuscript

One good way to read and appropriate a text carefully is to copy it in own's own handwriting. It then becomes "my" text, "our" text. If the passage to be studied is longer than three verses, all members of the group should first silently choose what seems to them to be the key verse and transform it from print into their own handwriting. This copy has to be double-checked against the printed text. In copying, we often write what we think should be there instead of what is really written. Such copying mistakes can be eye-openers to important unexpected details in the biblical text. After this individual work, the group discusses the key verses chosen and the insights gained by copying.

This exercise can also be done at the end of a Bible study. Participants are asked to write the key text of the passage studied on a small card, and to carry this with them and live with it through the week. It may happen that while reading the newspaper, doing the daily chores or talking with people at work or at home, one will discover new aspects of meaning in the verse which were not yet seen during the study group meeting.

Close reading

Text study makes us attentive to important details which are often overlooked.

For example, a careful reading of Mark 10:42-45 reveals much about how Jesus dealt with a situation of tension. Let the group first discover from the literary context what caused the tension between the disciples. Then ask the members in subgroups to examine step by step how Jesus approached and healed this situation. Close reading will reveal seven or even more subsequent steps in Jesus' "strategy" of dealing with such a crisis. Discoveries are then shared in plenary discussion.

For an examination of the Beatitudes in Matthew 5:3-11, ask such questions as the following:

What is the context of the Beatitudes? What comes in Matthew's gospel immediately before and after this text? At what stage of Jesus' ministry were the Beatitudes spoken, according to Matthew, and where did this happen? Look it up on a map of Palestine.

What are the key terms and the tenses of the verbs in the Beatitudes? Compare different translations of these key terms. To whom else in the gospels is the kingdom of heaven promised already now?

Compare Matthew's version of the Beatitudes with that of Luke 6:20-26. Do the details which differ teach us something about the two evangelists' special emphasis in their gospel?

Each of these three sets of questions can be assigned to a sub-group. These smaller groups then teach one another in the plenary.

The meaning of words

The above study on the Beatitudes can also be centred simply on the repeated expression: "Blessed are..." or "Happy are...". First compare different translations of this expression. Then teach the group about the meaning of the term *makarios* ("blessed" or "happy") in classical Greek, namely a life situation beyond all suffering and worry, such as that of the gods or of the deceased. Then let the group discover how the term "blessed" or "happy" is used in an Old Testament text by reading and discussing Psalm 1:1-3.

Clearly Jesus gave this term neither the classical Greek meaning nor exactly the Old Testament sense. Let sub-groups therefore discover what word or words might best paraphrase the meaning of *makarios*, as used in the Beatitudes. In the plenary session teach one another.

With the help of wordbooks, concordances and Bible encyclopaedias, animators can prepare many other similar word studies. Such terms as "salvation/liberation", "peace" and "fellowship" have many shades of meaning which lead to important biblical insights.

Working with a synopsis

For the study of gospel texts a synopsis is one of the best tools for literary comparison, close reading and discovering the evangelists' special emphases in their testimonies and "theologies".

To study Jesus' parable of the lost sheep try the following procedure:

First ask the group to reconstruct this well-known parable from memory, without looking in their Bibles. Participants should also try to remember the context in which Jesus taught the parable and to whom it was addressed. After ten minutes of recalling and talking it over with neighbours, ask several members to present their remembered version. This may lead to animated disagreements.

Next, hand out a worksheet on which Matthew 18:12-14 and Luke 15:3-7 are set side by side. Working with their neighbours or in sub-groups, group members should list all the similarities and differences between the two accounts and examine the different literary contexts and the different addressees.

This leads to discussion in the plenary of the specific styles of Matthew and Luke. This shows that the parable receives a different accentuation if spoken to the tax collectors and sinners (Luke 15:1), to the grumbling Pharisees and scribes (Luke 15:2) or to the disciples who worry about their attitude towards members of the fold who have gone astray (Matt. 18:1,15ff.). The study also illustrates how in the early church the original sayings and parables of Jesus were not only transmitted but applied and re-applied to new situations.

Similar synoptic studies can be made by juxtaposing different versions of other parables and sayings of Jesus. Compare for instance Matthew's and Luke's versions of the parable of the Great Supper (Matt. 22:1-14; Luke 14:15-24). Let the group discover Luke's narrative art, which enumerates concrete examples of the excuses given by the invited guests. Then help the group to decipher Matthew's more didactic version, which has the character of an allegory, in which at least some details point to layers of meaning and events beyond the immediate story: the meal foreshadows the messianic feast; the burning of the city may point to the destruction of Jerusalem in A.D. 70; the first two groups of messengers probably refer to the persecuted Old Testament prophets and the last messengers to the early Christian mission; the end of the story anticipates the final judgment.

More threatening to many group members will be the synoptic comparison of crucial events in Jesus' life and destiny, for instance, the scene in Gethsemane (compare Matthew's

account with John's testimony), or all four gospel accounts of
the crucifixion and resurrection. Participants will thereby have
to learn that the gospels are not history-writing in the modern
sense of this term but interpretative testimonies of events which
have happened, addressed to hearers and readers in different
situations. This may lead to teaching about the varying
"theologies" of the evangelists.

The Old Testament in the New

When studying an Old Testament text, it is always important to ask whether and how its affirmations have been taken
up and reinterpreted by New Testament witnesses. Conversely, while reading a New Testament text, one must always
be sensitive to its Old Testament background. The Old Testament emphasizes some affirmations more than the New Testament and vice-versa. Other insights can be gained only in either
the Old or the New Testament.

For a study of the last vision recorded in the Bible (Rev.
21:1-22:7), ask sub-groups to make a list of what they consider
the ten most important Old Testament texts quoted or clearly
alluded to here. These lists are compared and discussed in the
plenary. Then make a more thorough comparison between
Revelation 21:22-22:2 and Ezekiel 47:1-12. What are the
important similarities and differences?

Study Matthew's testimony about the death of Jesus (Matt.
27:45-54) in the light of Psalm 22. Let the group discover all
quotations from or references to this Psalm. If the crucifixion is
reported and understood in the light of Psalm 22, as Mark and
Matthew obviously did and as Jesus himself may have wanted
us to do, what light does the concluding part of this Psalm
throw on the meaning of Jesus' passion?

Not all evangelists have the same number of direct Old
Testament quotations. Matthew has many more than John.
However, counting quotations is not enough. The entire gos-
pel of John is in fact based on implicit references to Old
Testament themes and festivals. When studying John 7:37-39,
it is thus important to teach the group — or better to let the

group discover by reading Jewish texts — what happened on the last day of the feast of the tents.

Often there are also revealing allusions to deutero-canonical texts. Compare for instance John 1:1-18 with Sirach 24:3-12. Discover through group study the similarities and differences between the personified Wisdom in Sirach and the Word in John's prologue as well as their different "incarnations".

Distinguishing different literary genres

A poem must not be read like a legal text, nor a creed like a parable. It is important to distinguish such different literary genres in the Bible. Here are three exercises for such discernment:

Read one after another the three testimonies to God the Creator in Genesis 1:1-2:4a, Genesis 2:4b-25 and Psalm 8. The first has a repetitive, solemn, almost liturgical character and was probably written by priests. The second is clearly an ancient narrative account. The third is a poem of praise and teaching.

Read what Jotham told his brother Abimelech, who wanted to become a king, in Judges 9:8-15. What genre of literature is this? Read the context in which this was said and discuss its significance. What can it teach us about witness in present-day political power struggles?

Discover where the credal statements are in the two letters to Timothy. Study the affirmations of these statements and compare them with the Apostles' Creed.

Sensitivity to narrative structures and styles

Many biblical authors have artfully constructed their testimonies, for instance through "inclusions", in which the closing sentences take up the initial affirmations and give them a wider meaning. The biblical authors also have their own particular styles and sets of key terms.

The first title given to Jesus in Matthew's gospel is "Immanuel", "God with us". Luke's gospel begins with an unfinished worship service in the temple of Jerusalem, where the priest cannot give the final blessing. Have the group members examine the conclusions of these two gospels: In what way have the beginnings been taken up again and been expanded? What can we learn from these literary constructions about the main messages of the two gospels?

For a study of Jesus' trial before Pilate as recorded in John's gospel (18:28-19:16), have the group subdivide the passage into its seven sub-scenes and notice the constant change of actors and stages outside and inside the headquarters. What is the literary structure of this passage? Which sub-scene corresponds to which other? Which is the central sub-scene? Then help group members to discover the typical Johannine use of irony, double meanings of words, misunderstandings and reversals. Notice for example that the Jewish accusers who want to remain clean ultimately acknowledge not God but the Roman emperor as their lord. All through the passage Pilate becomes paradoxically the unwilling witness to Jesus (according to a possible translation of the Greek verb in 19:13, it is not he who sat on the judge's bench but he seated Jesus on it!); the king ("king" and "kingship" are used 12 times in this passage!) receives a crown of thorns.

Writing a letter

Studying Paul's letters is like listening to a telephone conversation in which one hears only one party. Like a detective one has to guess what the problems were which Paul addressed and what news he received to which he reacted.

Imagine what kind of letter Paul might have received from a frustrated member of the church among the Galatians. What was the gospel preachers from outside had been proclaiming after the apostle's departure? What had happened to the local church as a result? Paul obviously did not like this news and he immediately dictated an angry letter of response. This study of Galatians will take several sessions.

First let the group try to reconstruct the letter which Paul received and to which he responds. Begin by dividing the task among four sub-groups: the first reads Galatians 1-2, noting all the things to which Paul explicitly or implicitly reacts; a second does the same for 3:1-4:7; a third takes 4:8-5:1; a fourth 5:2-6:18. After about thirty minutes the group reassembles and makes a list of reports and questions to be included in the letter to be written. A drafter is then appointed.

In the next session the drafted letter is read aloud, and on the basis of Paul's letter to the Galatians the group examines how Paul responds. This may lead to many new questions, for Paul's arguments are often strange to us now. Already the early Christians found Paul sometimes "hard to understand" (2 Pet. 3:15-16). The participants may therefore want to write their own letter to Paul. For a closing session one can best invite someone who has studied Paul in depth. On the basis of the letters and questions received from the participants that scholar gives a presentation on Paul's theology.

III

The Bible as Drama

From text to celebration

The oral biblical testimonies were transmitted and fixed in writing in order to be celebrated, taught, proclaimed or used for apologetic purposes. The main reason for this transmission and writing down was the "remembering", the *anamnesis*. In the Bible "to remember" does not mean only to call to mind past events of salvation. It means actually to participate in them, to make them present and to re-enact them. "Remember this day," the Israelites assembled for worship were told: "You shall tell your child on that day: 'It is because of what the Lord did for me when *I* came out of Egypt'" (Ex. 13:8; compare Deut. 6:23). In the main old Jewish pilgrim festivals, the Passover and the feast of the tents (the *Sukkot*), the liberating events of their desert journey were dramatically remembered with readings, hymns, prayers, processions, tangible tokens and liturgical gestures. Such a making present of crucial moments of life and history also happened at the feasts which were established later such as the Day of Atonement *(Yom Kippur)*, Pentecost and the feast of dedication *(Hanukka)*.

To participate in these remembrances in the family and in the worship with sacrifices in the temple of Jerusalem was a powerful religious instruction and a dramatic Bible study. During the Passover meal the story of the exodus from Egypt was recalled and symbolically enacted. During the yearly pilgrimages to Jerusalem the songs of ascent (Pss. 120-134) were sung. It was mainly in this way that the boy Jesus learned about the faith of his ancestors.

The weekly worship in the synagogue had a more sober character than temple worship. Nevertheless, those attending were by no means passive spectators. The assembly described in Nehemiah 8:2-8, which anticipates later synagogue worship, shows this: the Torah is publicly shown to the assembly and the people stand as the scroll is opened. They join in the priest's blessing and praising God with the "Amen", lifting up their hands. Then they bow down to worship with their faces to the ground. This leads to the reading of the Torah, which is then interpreted to the people.

Remembering in Christian worship

Jewish synagogue worship left its mark on early Christian gatherings for worship. There was no fixed liturgy as yet; but although worship assemblies differed from place to place, the central act of remembering became the Lord's supper, the breaking of the bread. This was accompanied by reading the scriptures (the Old Testament) and learning what the apostles had taught — that is, their testimonies about Christ and about how the Old Testament should be understood in the light of Christ's coming. Such apostolic teaching was later fixed in writing in the New Testament. Prayer, hymns, spontaneous and often enthusiastic worship expressions characterized the whole (Acts 2:42, 46; 1 Cor. 11:20ff., 14:1ff.; 1 Tim. 4:13; and the book of Revelation, throughout which much of early Christian eucharistic worship echoes). Gradually, scripture passages for reading and interpretation were assigned to different seasons of the year. The Christian church also developed its own cycle of feasts. Sunday became the weekly remembrance of the day of resurrection. Then each year a season for remembering the death and resurrection of Jesus was set aside, followed later by yearly commemorations of the feasts of Pentecost, of Jesus' baptism and birth. From the fourth century onwards Christians began to make pilgrimages to Jerusalem and to the places where Jesus lived and taught.

Throughout the centuries the majority of Christians have come to know essential parts of the Bible by remembering the drama of salvation through Sunday worship, the feasts of the church year, pilgrimages and other acts of worship. In animating Bible studies one must always be aware of this age-old context of remembrance through worship.

From passion plays to biblio-drama

Both in the Orthodox churches of the East and in the churches of the West a rich liturgical worship developed. Worshippers in Orthodox churches have a strong conviction that they are participating here on earth in the ongoing heavenly liturgy with angels, martyrs, saints and believers of former ages. Church buildings, icons and a great deal of liturgical symbolism emphasize this heavenly worship. No wonder that the young son of one of my Orthodox colleagues once said to his father after attending a sober Protestant worship, "Daddy, I like our worship better: it looks better, sounds better, smells better and tastes better."

In the Western church from the ninth century onwards, the remembered events of salvation were actually dramatized on great feast days, especially at Easter. At first this happened very soberly through processions and dialogues within the liturgical framework. In the late middle ages Easter and Christmas plays began to be staged in monasteries and cathedrals, often still sung or chanted, but as separate celebrations alongside the normal liturgy. By the fourteenth century these became popular passion plays, re-enacting the whole drama of the passion week and Easter. The actors were now no longer priests and monks but lay people. The scene moved from the cathedral to the market place. Sometimes the passion plays were expanded with other scenes of Jesus' life. In the fifteenth century mystery plays lasting several days portrayed the entire history of salvation from creation to the final judgment.

Many of the mediaeval plays degenerated into cheap banter, losing their biblical content; and both the Reformers and the Jesuits opposed them vigorously. This does not take away the fact that in the middle ages large groups of people were confronted with essential biblical messages by acting in or attending such public dramas. The passion of Christ for them was not something that had taken place long ago and far away.

It happened in their own cities. Participating in a passion play never leaves one unchanged.

Some of this mediaeval biblical drama was revived in the eighteenth and nineteenth centuries, stimulated by the famous passion play in Oberammergau. During the twentieth century Christian youth groups have rediscovered the power of dramatization. There has been a growth of many biblical plays *(Laienspiele)*, not only at Christmas time but throughout the church year. Through street theatre such biblical plays have become a means of evangelization in several continents.

More recently, "biblio-drama" has been developed as an "existential" method of Bible study. It is derived from "psycho-drama" which is used in psychotherapy. Dramatized biblical stories are related with the life stories of the acting participants. Their present experiences of life help to interpret the Bible and vice-versa. The dramatized biblical passages throw new light on the life-situation and fundamental human questions of those who play in the biblio-drama.

The confrontation-play

A form of biblical dramatization which concentrates more than biblio-drama on reflection about the meaning of the biblical testimonies is the confrontation play. It passes through four stages: the introduction, the period of identification, the actual confrontation and, most important, the debriefing and reflection. The biblical passages which are most suitable for confrontation plays are those in which several clearly different persons and groups involved in different ways appear and there is some tension between the protagonists.

Introduction: Participants begin by reading the biblical passage to be studied and identifying the actors or groups of actors who play a role in it. Either through a worksheet or oral instruction information is given about the background of the reported events. Subsequently, participants are divided into as many sub-groups as there are actors in the story. Roles are assigned, preferably by drawing lots but in any case not by the animator. Usually it is better not to include Jesus and certainly not God among the roles to be taken. It must be made clear that in the period of confrontation what will be dramatized is not the biblical passage itself: the actors will meet only after the events reported have already taken place.

Identification: On the basis of the biblical passage, the different sub-groups try to identify themselves with their role (about 20 minutes). What did we (as Pharisees, women, passers-by) feel, see and say before, during and after the events reported? How did we relate to the other actors (including Jesus or God) before, during and after the events? The sub-groups should not prepare a script of what they are going to say but enter as fully as they can into the thinking and emotions of the person or group whom they represent.

Confrontation: Before the sub-groups are called together, the animator prepares the seating arrangement so that each of the sub-groups sits together, facing the group to whom, according to the biblical passage, they are most strongly opposed. When all have returned to their assigned places, the animator acts as an interested visitor arriving after the reported events took place, asking, "What has happened? Tell me." For 20-30 minutes the conversation and confrontation between the different sub-groups develop spontaneously. The animator intervenes by questions only if a particular sub-group is not getting a chance to speak or if necessary to reorient the confrontation to the main issues dealt with in the biblical passage. If the tension becomes too heavy for some (for instance, those who have to deride Jesus), participants who want to change roles must be given the chance to do so.

Debriefing and reflection: It is good to take a short break after the period of confrontation. For the next phase, participants must sit in a circle, but no longer beside members of their former sub-group. Most will find it difficult to liberate themselves from their role. It is best first to allow a chance for informal discussion among people seated next to each other about what they have experienced during the periods of identification and of confrontation. What did playing this role teach them about God, Jesus, Christian faith and themselves? This leads to a general discussion. Towards the end, the biblical passage is read again for checking which details, words and acts became especially important and which parts of the passage may have been neglected.

Symbolic acts and gestures

In all the preceding examples of dramatic Bible study words play an important role. However, tangible tokens, symbolic actions and silent gestures can also become powerful media of learning and remembering. Joshua not only wrote the words of the covenant in a book but also set up a large stone as a token and witness to it (Josh. 24:26f., cf. 4:20ff.). During the Passover meals several such tangible tokens, symbols and gestures form an integral part of the celebration. At some of the most crucial moments of his ministry and teaching Jesus said little or nothing, but taught by significant gestures.

The power of such non-verbal remembering has not been forgotten in church history. A third-century baptismal liturgy from the church in Rome illustrates this. The persons who were baptized there spoke little during the ceremony, but their being accepted into the church became for them an unforgettable death-and-life experience, a desertion from the army of Satan and an incorporation into the army of Christ. They would never forget the night-long vigil, the "burial" into flowing water, the ritual of exorcism, the white garments, the anointing with the oil of thanksgiving, the kiss of peace and their first participation in the eucharist. Paul's baptismal teaching in Romans 6:1-11 must have been very much on their minds.

In Bible study attention to such non-verbal ways of communication is important. What tangible tokens, movements of the actors, body attitudes and gestures can we observe in a given biblical passage? How can we enact a biblical story without speaking or while someone is reading the story slowly? In chapter V we shall discuss the highly meditative way of miming, which is much more than silent enacting.

Suggestions for Bible Studies Based on Drama

Re-enacting a Psalm

Many of the Psalms are directly related to community worship in homes, at festivals and in the temple. Simply to read them individually and silently does not do justice to their origin, purpose and form. Even responsive reading or recitation by two groups which alternately read one verse — as is often done in public worship — can blind us to the real movements, drama and climaxes in the text.

Read Psalm 24 with a group, then ask the following questions:

Who speaks in this Psalm? Is it one person or a whole assembly or perhaps alternately an individual and a group?

Examine carefully the verbs used and discover the successive body postures, gestures and movements of the worshippers in this Psalm.

On the basis of the worshippers' attitudes and movements, envisage the original localities and improvize a stage for enacting.

These three tasks can best be done first by buzz-groups, each time followed by plenary discussion in which insights are shared and one of the suggested answers is chosen for enactment. After the group has decided on the actors, the movements and the stage, the study is best concluded with a re-enactment of the Psalm.

Similar studies can be done with other Psalms. For example, let the group discover who is speaking in Psalm 95, what movements can be seen and why the whole atmosphere changes in the middle of verse 7. Probably a prophet interrupted a joyful but hypocritical worship procession, as Amos once did in Bethel (Amos 7:10-17). Let the group transpose this Psalm for their own time and their own worship assemblies. What would the prophet have to say today? Then re-enact Psalm 95 in this modern version.

Studies by confrontation plays

A good text to learn by conducting a confrontation play is Mark 2:1-12. During the introductory period it is helpful to share some information about flat-roof houses in Palestine (possibly by showing photographs), in order to visualize the setting. Also some teaching will be needed concerning the convictions of scribes and Pharisees about the forgiveness of sins. During the periods of identification and confrontation, the participants divide into four sub-groups, taking the roles of the crowd, the paralytic, the friends of the paralytic and the scribes respectively. In the period of reflection, some teaching about the title "Son of Man" will be needed.

Certain incidents in the life and ministry of the Old Testament prophets also lend themselves to confrontation plays, especially if the prophetic message is communicated through a prophetic act, for example, the confrontation between Jeremiah carrying the yoke and Hananiah (Jer. 27:1, 28:1-17). Among New Testament passages, this dramatic method can be used for a study of the letter to Philemon. Confrontation plays also offer a way into a profound understanding, with both mind and heart, of scenes from the passion stories, the religious and political power play behind the events, the fear of the disciples and the courage of the women. Something of the mystery of the resurrection can be grasped by studying Matthew 27:62–28:10 through such a play.

Discovering the message of gestures

Many books have been written about the sayings of the prophets and Jesus. Especially in literary cultures it is important to counterbalance this emphasis on the spoken message by developing sensitivity to symbolic acts and gestures. After a Bible study group has spent several sessions studying the words of the prophets and the sayings of Jesus, the following series of studies might be done:

Using historical-literary methods, examine a prophetic act, for instance the one recorded in 1 Kings 11:29-39. Then assign to each member of the group one of the following chapters from the Old Testament prophetic books as homework: Isaiah 7, 8, 20; Jeremiah 13, 16, 19, 27, 28, 32, 43, 51; Ezekiel 4, 5, 12, 21, 24, 37. The task is to discover the prophetic signs in the assigned chapter and to prepare a short description of such prophetic acts, their original circumstances and their messages. In the succeeding sessions of the study group these various prophetic acts are presented and discussed. Concluding this series, the group should attempt to discover necessary prophetic acts for their own time and environment.

After a short introduction on prophetic signs, allow sub-groups 30 minutes to discover as many significant gestures in the life and ministry of Jesus as they can find in the gospels. When the group reassembles the discoveries are shared. One or several of these gestures of Jesus may then be studied more thoroughly in subsequent sessions.

The original meaning of the Lord's supper

Even though members of the Orthodox, Roman Catholic and Protestant churches cannot yet fully share in one another's eucharistic celebrations, they can study together what the gospel writers and Paul wrote about the origin of the Lord's supper. This study can best be conducted in the following way.

Begin by having the participants recall, with their Bibles closed, the circumstances, time, locality and participants of the institution of the Lord's supper; the elements used; the gestures Jesus made during the institution; and the words he spoke in connection with these elements and gestures. Most will accurately remember the elements and the gestures, but will understandably have difficulty remembering the exact words.

Then distribute a worksheet with a synopsis of Matthew 26:26-29, Mark 14:22-25, Luke 22:15-20 and 1 Corinthians 11:23-26. Working preferably in sub-groups, the participants should identify and discuss all the similarities and differences. In doing so, they will notice that in all of the accounts the elements and gestures are the same or almost the same. We have here an accurate and clearly remembered part of the original event. How are the differences with regard to the sayings to be explained? Here we may have remembrances of different ways in which the early church celebrated the Lord's supper, for instance among Judaeo-Christians in Palestine and among the local churches which grew out of Paul's missionary work. Almost certainly, different interpretations of the meaning of the Lord's supper appear here as well.

A crucial question: "What was Jesus referring to when he said: 'This is...'?" Most group members will probably answer, "The elements — the bread and wine." This is not wrong, but the reference probably embraces more, possibly in the first place the gestures of breaking and pouring out. The Greek text of the four accounts points to this wider meaning: the "this" (*touto* in Greek) is neuter, while "bread" (*artos* in Greek) is masculine. For the evangelists and Paul to refer with a neuter pronoun to a masculine noun would have been bad grammar, but *touto* can very well point to the series of gestures and the elements together.

A final question: "What did Jesus mean when he said: 'Do this'"? Many participants will answer: "He wanted us to continue the celebration of the Lord's supper." Again, this is probably part of the meaning. However, the words can also point beyond the liturgy to the whole of life. Time was running out, and the disciples had not yet fully understood the ministry for which Jesus had come. During this last meal with them, Jesus therefore summed up his whole ministry with a series of prophetic gestures and words: "This is... This, in a nutshell, is what I came for. This is the pattern of my life: to receive from God's creation and human work the bread, everyday food in Palestine, and the wine, the drink for feasts, to lift up my hands for blessing and thanking God, to be broken as bread is broken and to shed my blood 'for you' as wine is poured out, to be given and be spent. Now 'do this': enter into the pattern of my life." In the parallel text of John 13:1-17 the "do this" refers to the gesture of washing the feet and not to the element of water.

Jesus there calls on the disciples to live according to the example given and the pattern set. Similarly, the institution of the Lord's supper calls for a whole eucharistic life, which again and again is signified to us through eucharistic celebrations.

This study can best conclude by having the members of the group join in a silent participation in the eucharistic gestures of Jesus. Ask them to stand and, together with the animator, consecutively make the gestures of receiving, blessing and thanking God, breaking and being broken, of shedding and being shed and finally of giving, of sharing oneself with others.

IV

The Bible as the Visible Word

From the ear to the eye

There is little abstract language in the Bible and no definitions. Verbs predominate over nouns. Biblical language has sometimes been described as "theopoetic", poetry about God. How could one speak about God other than through a language which evokes realities rather than describing and delimiting them? When Jesus spoke about God's coming reign, he said, "The kingdom of God is like..." — and then told a parable, gave a word-image or made a visible gesture directing our eyes to ordinary things: a sower, a woman preparing bread, a mustard seed, children quarrelling on the village square. He challenged us to look at the ordinary things of earthly reality and to discern their depth-dimensions which point to God's reality.

In the Bible the relationship between hearing and seeing, between the word and the image, is a complex one. No one can see God and live. Yet at times this elusive God yields to the human desire to see the divine. There are theophanies, manifestations of God's presence and glory. When Moses insisted on knowing God's design and seeing God's face, he had to be content with the assurance that God knew him. Only from a protected cleft in the rock could he see God's back (Ex. 33:1-23). While there is no direct seeing of God, some visible signs of God's presence are given. The second of the ten commandments (Ex. 20:4ff.) is not a prohibition of art and artifacts, as Jews and Christians have often thought. Exodus 35:30ff. and the many artistic designs and objects in the temple of Jerusalem show that what is prohibited is idolatry, not art.

In the New Testament the same complex relation between seeing and hearing appears. When Thomas wanted to see the risen Lord, he was told: "Blessed are those who have not seen and yet have come to believe" (John 20:29). "Faith comes from what is heard, and what is heard comes through the word of Christ" (Rom. 10:17). These and similar texts give hearing precedence over seeing. Yet in Jesus the distorted image of God has been restored and can be seen by those who have eyes of faith. "We have seen his glory," testifies John (John 1:14; cf. 1 John 1:1); and Paul defends his apostleship with the exclamation: "Have I not seen Jesus our Lord?" (1 Cor. 9:1). Jesus himself affirmed: "Whoever has seen me has seen the Father" (John 14:9). Nevertheless, such seeing of God in the earthly Jesus is only for those who can recognize God's glory in the humiliation of Jesus on the cross. Once, three disciples saw the glory of Jesus on the mountain of transfiguration, but even on that occasion the accent was put more on hearing than on seeing: "Listen to him!" the divine voice commanded (Mark 9:7). Seeing is always only an anticipation of what is to come. When there is a new heaven and a new earth, then God's servants will "see his face" (Rev. 22:4).

The struggle about images in church history

The Jews and Christians of the first centuries of our era lived in an idolatrous society in which many images were worshipped — representations of divinities, the statues of divinized Caesars and altars for emperor-worship. The beginnings of both Jewish and Christian art were therefore slow and controversial, and ever since that time, iconoclastic movements have periodically challenged the legitimacy of pictorial representations of the divine.

The fierce struggle between attackers and defenders of icons in the Eastern church led in A.D. 787 to the decisions of the seventh ecumenical council in Nicaea. Icons are "useful in many respects, but especially in this, that thus the incarnation of the word of God is shown forth as real and not merely imaginary". When the worshippers see the cross and holy images in the church, in homes and by the wayside, they are "lifted up to the memory of their prototypes, and to a longing after them. To these [the cross and the icons] should be given due salutation and honourable reverence *(proskynesis)*, not indeed that true worship of faith *(latreia)* which pertains alone to the divine nature."

The statement of a later council in 860 said: "What the gospel tells us by words, the icon proclaims by colours and makes it present for us."

In the Western church Christian art developed originally against the resistance of the highly literate church fathers. However, the influx of illiterate tribes from northern and eastern Europe into the relatively literate Roman civilization made biblical art necessary, mainly for pedagogical reasons. Around the year 600 Pope Gregory the Great wrote: "Images are for unlettered beholders what scripture is for the reader."

During the Reformation iconoclastic movements arose mainly in reaction to the worship of relics, statues of Mary and saints in the popular Catholicism of that time. The attitudes among the Reformers themselves differed. Luther, a friend and neighbour of the painter Lucas Cranach, knew that we cannot really think without visualizing our thoughts. He appreciated art, but the image had to be shaped and interpreted by the word of God. As such Luther accepted the pedagogical use of images for Christian education (compare his Passion booklet of 1545). He helped Cranach in designing painted altar pieces and fostered the polemic use of caricatures. Zwingli, the humanist, enjoyed art but saw no use for images in Christian worship. Calvin accepted sculptured and painted representations of natural beauty as gifts of God if used for God's glory. He spoke against the destruction of works of art but did not tolerate them in church buildings. According to him only words and not images could communicate something divine.

This strong insistence on the word of God led in later Protestant orthodoxy to what might almost be called a "logo-latry" (a false worship of words, especially of dogmatic formu-lations), similar to the idolatry of images in other periods of church history. Nevertheless, there were some great biblical interpreters among Protestant artists, of whom the greatest was undoubtedly Rembrandt; and there are signs in our time that the estrangement between Protestantism and the artists may be overcome.

Artists as popular interpreters of the Bible

The earliest Christian art — paintings in the catacombs, sculptures on stone coffins (sarcophagi) and frescoes found in Dura-Europos on the Euphrates — date from the third century. It is mainly symbolic, using much typology, but portrayals of biblical scenes also appear. From the fourth century onwards, biblical manuscripts were often illuminated by colourful representations of biblical stories. On a twelfth-century scroll from southern Italy, the biblical text is written on one side for the priest to read aloud, while pictorial representations of the biblical text are painted on the other side, where they would be visible to the congregation: an early use of the audio-visual medium. Increasingly, artists had become the popular interpreters of the Bible, transforming mediaeval cathedrals through their sculptures, frescoes and stained-glass windows into "Bibles in stone and glass".

The most striking example of visual biblical teaching and learning is the *Biblia pauperum*. These compendiums of biblical stories and theology began to circulate in Germany from 1300 onwards. They were used by mendicant friars and village priests for popular teaching. In 34 scenes from the New Testament, beginning with the Annunciation and ending with Pentecost and the non-biblical scene of Mary's coronation, the whole drama of salvation was shown through a visual typological presentation. Each gospel episode is surrounded by four prophets who announce the gospel event and by two Old Testament scenes functioning as anticipatory types. Only very few explanatory words are added to the drawings. Those who looked at these small booklets, memorizing them visually, saw the Bible as a whole. Their theology was obviously that of late mediaeval Catholicism.

In the contemporary world we are constantly bombarded by evocative images through the mass media, often communicating horror or a gospel of pleasure and self-satisfaction. Studies which make us sensitive to the imagery of the Bible are a good antidote to passive consumption of ever new images. They also help us not to become cynical and not to succumb to shallow gospels. We must learn to see again. Artists can help us in this, for as the Swiss painter Paul Klee said, "art does not reproduce the visible, but it makes visible". It opens up and points to deeper meanings. In this sense artists often function as prophets. All true art — and not only "religious art" or art based on biblical stories and themes — can help in participatory Bible study.

Working with visual media and art

Visual media for group Bible study have become popular: flannelgraph, photo-collage, slides, overhead projectors, films and videos. For many regions of the world such media are too expensive. Moreover, if the room has to be darkened eye-to-eye contact is hindered. The use of such media also risks diverting the participants' attention away from the biblical messages to the medium. Therefore, the simplest media still remain the best for participatory study. Among these, "photo-language" and drawing have proved to stimulate the most visual creativity.

For working with photo-language, one needs a set of fairly large black-and-white photographs or photocopies of them: evocative human faces; children, young and old people of different races in happy and sad life situations; ordinary scenes from daily life with several people, animals and objects; landscapes or semi-abstract subjects and the like. With such a set of images it is usually easy to get all members of a group to participate in the discussion.

One possible way of proceeding is as follows. The group first carefully reads a biblical passage, examines its context and is given explanations about any difficult expressions in it. Then the animator spreads a set of photographs widely over the floor. Group members circulate and look silently at the photographs without picking them up. Most if not all of the participants will gradually discover a link between one or another photograph and the biblical passage which was studied. When all the group members have seen all the photographs and most have selected one of them, they pick up "their" photograph and go into small sub-groups. If several members have chosen the same photograph they form a sub-group together. There they listen and tell one another why this photograph has spoken to them and what light this has shed on the biblical passage. Some of these comments are then shared with the whole group.

An even better visual medium is the oldest of all — drawing. Not everyone is an artist, but anyone can draw after some practice. One needs only a finger and some sandy ground or a chalk and a blackboard (better than paper and marking pens, because what is drawn can easily be wiped out or changed). The "talk and chalk" method leads to much participation. A biblical passage is examined by the group and several questions are posed to them: How could this or that key term in the passage best be visualized and drawn? How can the drawing visualize the movements in the passage and the sequence of the sub-scenes? How might the main affirmation of the whole passage be visualized? While the group comments on these questions, one or more members draw, erase and draw again as interesting new suggestions are made by the group. The drawing thus constantly changes and develops.

For many people a striking drawing, painting or sculpture enters deeply into their sub-conscious and becomes part of their frame of reference. This can have good or bad consequences. For example, if children and adults have always seen Jesus as a blond, white European, it will be difficult for them to realize that Jesus was a brown-skinned Semite. Sunday school pictures imported from the West have created many misunderstandings about Jesus and Christian faith in Africa and other continents. Art work based on biblical scenes by Asian and African artists can therefore help both people in their own cultures and people of the North Atlantic world to challenge unconscious presuppositions.

All good art, whether or not it is outspokenly religious or biblical, can help to start or conclude the study of a biblical passage or theme. Silently looking at such a piece of art and letting it speak to us calls on ways of understanding other than only intellectual ones. Group members who speak the least often during an historical-literary study will frequently have the deepest insights to contribute while working with visual art.

Suggestions for Studies of the Visible Word

Silent dialogues

An excellent way to stimulate imagination and sensitivity to a partner is the "silent dialogue". Each member of the group sits opposite another member with a piece of paper between them. They decide to have an exchange about, for example, "children". From then onwards they take turns drawing on the paper without speaking. One starts with a small fragment, simply a point or a line. The other adds another line or an angle. For the first few minutes, neither knows what the other wants to say by such fragments of an envisaged drawing, and there is much guessing. Often one partner, discerning the drawing envisaged by the other, has to abandon his or her own concept. Gradually, a fairly chaotic drawing appears, which may reveal either a growing mutual understanding or a persistent misinterpretation of the partner's concept. Only then do the two speak with one another and explain what they wanted to draw and how they understood or misunderstood the partner.

For Bible study such silent dialogues can best be done on such themes as "covenant", "exile", "forgiveness" or "hope". After the silent dialogue, a text study is done on the chosen theme.

Drawing biblical images, texts and symbols

Biblical language calls for visualization. Word-images and symbols have their own way of communicating. Simply talking about them and explaining them intellectually risks impoverishing their messages. They must be drawn and looked at.

In the New Testament one finds no definitions of the church, but many images are given of Christian community — such as "You are the salt of the earth". Begin by having participants work for 30 minutes in sub-groups, looking for as many images for Christian community as possible in the gospels and the rest of the New Testament and immediately drawing them on a large sheet of paper. When the whole group reassembles each sub-group presents the New Testament images for the church which they found (there are in fact almost a hundred such images, many of them only minor variations of several major image-groups). All then look at the images found and drawn with this question in mind: "What do these images teach us about the nature of the church and its mission in the world?" This leads to general discussion. If time allows, participants go back into sub-groups to search for and draw new images of the church which are not in the Bible and which would speak strongly to people of today without betraying what can be learned from the biblical images.

Drawing can also be used for the close reading of a text. Let a group study Acts 2:36-38 in order to answer the question, "What must happen according to this text before a person can be baptized?" By "talk and chalk" the conditions for baptism are then discovered and fixed by drawing: the proclamation that the crucified Jesus is Lord and Messiah; the hearing of this message; hearts being pierced by what is heard; the questioning of the direction of one's life and repenting. Then follows the question: "What does baptism mean and effect according to this text?" Let the group discover by "talk and chalk" several ways to visualize the receiving of forgiveness of sins and of the Holy Spirit.

Symbols are visual confessions of faith. Once in East Java, Indonesia, a group of Hindu, Muslim and Christian students asked me to animate an inter-religious spiritual retreat. The purpose was not to make a mixture of different beliefs but to come to know the other's faith and mutually to testify to one's own deep convictions. The programme for this retreat in a secluded place consisted mainly of long periods of silence. The only input was three sessions: one led by a Hindu student who drew Hindu symbols, commenting on them in the light of Hindu scriptures; a second led by a Muslim student who drew Muslim symbols and commented on them based on the Qur'an; a third led by a Christian student drawing Christian symbols and commenting on them on the basis of the Bible. This led to a good deal of mutual understanding, a true testimony of faith and deepening of spiritual life. In a similar way, drawing Christian symbols — for instance, various forms of the cross — and reflecting on them in the light of central biblical messages can become a deeply meaningful Bible study.

Preparing meditations with photo-language

In addition to the way of working with photo-language mentioned earlier, one can give each sub-group a set of about six photographs chosen at random. Each of them also receives the same very short biblical text — a verse from a Psalm, one of the Beatitudes or one of the "I am"-sayings of Jesus in John's gospel. The task for the sub-groups is to prepare within 30 minutes a short audio-visual meditation on this text. They may use not more than three of the photographs, and for each photograph the text of the meditation may be no longer than fifteen or twenty words. The aim is not to "illustrate" the text with the photographs but to allow the images to speak in their own right. Usually the meditation gains depth if a certain tension remains between what the images convey and what the spoken meditation says. The group then assembles to see and hear these meditations and to ponder them.

Conceiving a page of the *Biblia pauperum*

If possible, distribute a worksheet with a photocopied reproduction of a page of the *Biblia pauperum*, for instance, the scene of the birth of Jesus. Let the group discover what the prophets say (in one version of the *Biblia pauperum* they point to texts like Isa. 9:6, Micah 5:2 and Dan. 2:34) and what the two Old Testament types are (in the same manuscript they represent Moses near the burning bush and Aaron with his blossoming staff, Ex. 3; Num. 17). The group is thus familiarized with the pedagogical way in which a page of the *Biblia pauperum* brings together the Old and the New Testaments. (Understanding the peculiar late mediaeval theology behind it will be much more difficult, but that is not necessary for this exercise.) Sub-groups are then formed for the following task: Try to conceive and create a *Biblia pauperum* page on Pentecost. Draw in the centre of a sheet the New Testament Pentecost scene. What four Old Testament prophecies could figure in it (simply write the first words of each prophecy)? Which two Old Testament scenes could function as types for Pentecost (make a simple drawing of these scenes)? At the end, the sub-groups gather, show one another their work and discuss what they have learned about typological exegesis and about Pentecost.

Learning from artists

A visit to a mediaeval cathedral with a good guide or looking together at reproductions from illuminated biblical manuscripts can become a Bible study which opens up many insights. One discovers the influence that typological exegesis and apocryphal gospels had in the middle ages.

A good way to link art and the Bible is to look at some modern secular art works and to ask which biblical themes and affirmations they express, even if the artist may not have thought of these.

To discover that biblical events must be reinterpreted again and again for new times and cultures, one can use slides to show how artists have portrayed the crucifixion in different centuries and cultural environments. Such a slide series opens the eyes to the various ways in which the evangelists and other New Testament authors were already both transmitting and interpreting the event of crucifixion. This visual presentation can function either as the introduction to or conclusion of a series of text studies on the crucifixion.

For meditations using Orthodox icons see the next chapter.

V

Meditation on the Bible

"The Bible is food for wrestlers," D.T. Niles, the Sri Lankan biblical teacher, once said. It is not for those who simply gather in pious circles to edify themselves, but for those who are engaged in a struggle of prayer and in the battles of faith in the world. To do Bible study simply for the sake of Bible study soon becomes stale. Conversely, those involved in struggles need nourishing and well-digested food. It is neither the amount of food we eat nor the amount of biblical knowledge we acquire that feeds us. It is the amount we digest. Meditating on the Bible is an essential part of this necessary digesting.

From the ear to the heart

There are many ways of biblical meditation, most of which involve the practice of individual daily Bible reading and prayer. The *lectio divina*, the "Moravian watchwords" and the "morning watch" are typical examples of these.

The *lectio divina* is based on what Jews and Christians practised already in biblical times, and it became an integral part of monastic life. It consists of a daily attempt to listen to God's word within a prescribed biblical text. This happens at regular hours according to a lectionary which covers the whole Bible, so that for example the whole book of Psalms or all four gospels are read consecutively. Sensitivity to resonances from the whole Bible is needed so that the scripture itself interprets the meditated scripture passage and so that God's word heard shapes human thought and life. This meditation passes through four stages:

The reading of the text of the day, reread several times, so that it is memorized.

Meditation on the text, so that one penetrates to the particular meaning and the messages of God's word which are to be heard.

Prayer in silence, becoming a very personal dialogue with God.

Contemplation, which often leads only to emptiness but remains open for moments of grace when those who meditate are surprised by the joy of God's presence and when God's word questions, hurts and heals their heart and directs their life.

Other ways of daily reading and meditating are more adapted to the life of lay people in the world. Since the 1730s the Moravian Church has issued daily meditation texts: Old Testament verses selected by lot, each linked with a specially chosen New Testament text and a verse of a hymn which prolong and inform the meditation. Ever since these "Moravian watchwords" have been published, they have nourished and guided believers for their everyday life in many confessions and on all continents.

During the great revival movements of the nineteenth century the "morning watch" became for many Christians a daily moment of biblical meditation within their busy life in the world. Several international Bible reading associations, Christian movements and churches began to provide lectionaries and short daily text meditations in different languages and for various age groups. Especially in ecumenical youth movements, the YMCA, YWCA and the World Student Christian Federation, this "morning watch" was faithfully kept until the turmoils of twentieth-century history let it weaken and disappear in many places.

If at least some members of a Bible study group keep up the discipline of such daily individual biblical meditation, the work and insights gained in that group will be greatly enriched. However, there are many — including the author — who have neither the discipline nor the type of spirituality to enter daily and alone at a regular hour into the necessary silence for meditatively hearing God's word in the Bible. So here are some ways of biblical meditation which can occasionally be practised in a group. They all involve the mysterious reversal of roles that can happen in Bible study, about which the African woman quoted in the introduction spoke. This is always risky, for it might convert us and change the direction of our lives.

A fantasy journey

Mediaeval artists often included a small portrait of themselves in a corner of their painting, thus becoming part of their work of art. Similarly, an essential aspect of meditation is to try to become part of the biblical story and event. One has to imagine being there, hearing inwardly what is being said, seeing what is happening — even to the extent of seeing oneself there and hearing oneself addressed. A "fantasy journey" can be helpful for this. Most gospel stories, as well as prophetic visions of the Old Testament and the dramatic scenes of John's Revelation, lend themselves well to such meditation.

For some participants, however, a fantasy journey can become a traumatic experience. At the very outset it must therefore be made clear that everyone should feel free to join or not to join in the journey, to come along simply as a spectator or to identify with a person or group of the story. Many will follow the journey only up to a certain point and then stop, drift away or even fall asleep. It is good to mention all this so that no one needs to feel awkward during the meditation.

A secluded place and a considerable amount of mutual confidence between the animator and the group are needed. Sometimes it is helpful to show a photograph of the place where the biblical story or vision originally happened and to explain the meaning of certain words and symbols which play an important role in the biblical passage. Such background information must be short and should not limit the imaging of the participants.

In preparation for the journey participants are asked to sit upright on a chair or lie down on the floor so that they can breathe quietly and remain still for about 20 minutes. Then they are asked to close their eyes, keeping them closed during the whole journey, and to visualize internally what will be said. Sometimes it helps this internal visualization for the animator to lead the participants in their imagination first to a place of their own time and environment which resembles the original setting of the biblical story or vision. After this those who meditate are invited to a journey through time and space. Some meditative music, for instance by a flute, helps many on this journey towards the original time and place of the biblical story or vision.

Once they arrive there, the music fades away. The animator describes with few concrete details the initial scene where the story or vision begins: the place, the persons, the atmosphere. Then the story or vision is told in a quiet voice, with many pauses, so that the participants can follow the action without hurry and have time to visualize what happens in each new scene. The story or vision must be told as nearly as possible to the biblical text, without additions and embellishments.

After a moment of quiet at the end, the animator asks participants to return slowly from the biblical time and place into the here and now. Again some flute music may help this return. Only then are the group members invited to open their eyes, look around and stretch their bodies.

The follow-up of a fantasy journey depends a great deal on the composition of the group, the time available and the place of the meditation. Participants might be asked to go first for an individual walk, recalling the story or vision and meditating on it as they do. They then gather again and tell one another what they have experienced and what insights they have gained. Or participants can be invited to respond to the passage they have meditated on by writing a prayer or a poem, or expressing it through a body movement. These responses are then brought before God and before the group in a moment of worship. A third way to follow up is first to ask participants to share with the neighbours sitting besides them what they have experienced during the journey. Then the text is read again and examined. What was emotionally experienced and understood is checked, corrected and complemented by the intellectually understood meaning of the story or vision.

Miming the message

One of the most meditative ways of Bible study is miming. We reflect and understand not only with our mind and intellect and we communicate not only with our words and writings. In a very deep way we can reflect, understand and communicate with our body — through its posture, through its movement or simply through an expressive gesture with our hands. The deepest feelings of love and sorrow are often better expressed through a look in our eyes, a touch or a silent gesture than through words. Our bodies are privileged media of communication, and they can in a literal sense "incorporate" a message. Too often Christians have ignored Paul's question and exhortation: "Do you not know that your body is the temple of the Holy Spirit within you, which you have from God?... Therefore glorify God in your body" (1 Cor. 6:19). The neglect of this insight leaves the way wide open for what unfortunately often happens: the body is either adored and divinized or despised and demonized. In either case the body loses its primary function as a medium for relationships, reflection and understanding, a way of expressing our communion with the created world, with fellow human beings and with God.

Just as true art does not simply reproduce what is immediately visible but makes visible the meaning behind the superficial appearance, so mime is not mimicry. It makes visible through body movement what has been seen inwardly and deeply understood. It is nearer to poetry than to theatre.

A meditative way to explore the message in a biblical passage is thus to transform it into a mime, either individually or as a group. Poetic and reflective texts are best suited for such bodily meditation. If stories and other narrative texts are portrayed in this way, they tend too easily to become over-dramatic and ridiculous. A passage can be mimed only if one has penetrated to its heart, to its basic postures, movement and message. All additional and secondary details must be left aside. The simpler and better coordinated the movement is, the more impressive and memorable the mime becomes. Such meditation through miming is an intimate exercise. It can be done only in a secluded and quiet place, with groups in which there is much mutual confidence. The most congenial environment for miming is worship or a spiritual retreat. Unless thoroughly practised, biblical mimes should never be "performed" before a public.

For people and groups who have never done meditative miming, some preliminary exercises are needed. Ask participants to imagine that they are on a seashore collecting shells, or that they are throwing small pebbles into the water or lifting a heavy stone. The shells or stones are simply imagined and the movements made as if they were in the participants' hands. Then ask members of the group to become "statues", assuming a body attitude which expresses waiting, fear, sorrow, joy or hope. After this some transformations should be attempted — for example, changing from a "statue" of fear to one of joy. In group mimes it is important to do exercises in which two partners move together: one making various body movements, the other responding with his or her body without the two touching each other. The roles are then reversed. Two partners can also try to express with body postures a situation in which one is an oppressor and the other oppressed. Then they seek a movement which shows how both oppressor and oppressed are being liberated.

Many participants may find it too threatening to mime with their whole body. Miming simply with one's hands while remaining seated may be more acceptable. As a preliminary exercise, participants might be asked to show with movements how one hand accepts or rejects the other, or how one hand liberates the other which is tightly closed. Such hand-mimes can also be done together with a partner.

Only when group members have discovered the possibilities of mime and the marvellous medium of their bodies can this way of expression be applied to biblical meditation.

The *ruminatio*

The Hebrew word usually translated "to meditate" means literally "to murmur in a low voice". Psalm 1:1-2 calls on us to do so. Mary must have used this Jewish way of meditation when she "treasured up in her heart" and "pondered" what the angel and then the boy Jesus had said (Luke 2:19,51). What has been heard, memorized and internalized must be recalled and recited for oneself again and again.

The church fathers developed the idea and practice of *ruminatio* on the basis of an allegorical interpretation of the rumination of animals who were believed to be clean (Deut. 14:6). The early fourth-century Egyptian hermit St Anthony used the following humorous comparison:

> A camel needs only a little food; it keeps it within until it returns to the stable. It lets the food come up again and ruminates it until the food enters the camel's bones and flesh. The horse, however, needs much food; it eats all the time and soon loses all it has eaten. So let us not be like a horse, continuously reciting the words of God without obeying them. Let us rather resemble the camel, reciting each word of God and retaining it within us until we have lived it.

St Anthony was emphasizing here the intimate relationship between the act of ruminating and its consequence: of being penetrated by God's word to such an extent that it shapes our actions. Other authors describe the *ruminatio* more in terms of meditation which leads to new insights and continuous prayer. In his *Discipline for the Life of Ministers*, Martin Luther offered this advice:

> In the evening, as you go to bed, by all means take a passage of the holy scripture with you, know it by heart, and when you ruminate on it, you quickly fall asleep like a pure animal. This passage must not be too copious, but rather brief, yet well meditated and understood. And as you awake in the morning, you must find it back, like an inheritance from the past evening.

Ruminatio is usually done as a form of personal biblical meditation, but it can also be done in group work. In this case, each participant must first write the short biblical passage for meditation in his or her own handwriting on a piece of paper. The animator may make a few explanatory comments on the literary and historical context of the passage and explain the meaning of any unfamiliar terms. To imprint the text on the memory, it is then read aloud several times by individuals and by the whole group. The wording (though not the content) may need to be altered slightly so that the reading aloud becomes rhythmic and can be easily recited while walking.

After this introductory work together, each group member goes walking for about half an hour, constantly murmuring the memorized passage according to the rhythm of his or her steps. While walking and ruminating he or she looks around, seeing the everyday sights of the landscape and human life. In this process the walkers may become spontaneously aware of relationships between the text on which they are ruminating and the things and persons they see. Rather than a printed exposition, it is God's creation and everyday human life which become the biblical commentary. This leads to new insights both about the passage and about oneself and one's life in this world. Such an exercise can best be concluded by having the participants come back together in the group and try to formulate the insights they have gained in a few sentences, a prayer or a poem, which they share with the others.

The painted prayers of icons

The term "icon" (Greek *eikōn*) evokes several biblical passages and convictions. The first is the fundamental affirmation that human beings have been created in the image and likeness of God (Gen. 1:26f., 5:1f., 9:6; Sirach 17:3). Second, there is the conviction that the distorted image of God has become visible again in Jesus Christ (Col. 1:15; 2 Cor. 4:4; cf. John 12:45). Third, the belief is expressed that our true identity as God's image is being recovered in us if we live in communion with Christ (1 Cor. 15:49; Rom. 8:29; 2 Cor. 3:18); we are being transformed ("metamorphosed" in Greek) into his *eikōn* or image. Just as the biblical term *eikōn* points to the intimate relationship between human beings and God, so Byzantine and Orthodox icons are painted prayers, helps for meditation, for strengthening our relationship with God.

For groups who have never meditated with icons, it is best to invite a member of an Orthodox church to explain what the icons in the home and the church mean to him or her. Icons must not be looked at as if they were Renaissance art. An ancient Orthodox liturgical manual advises: "In order to learn iconography and understand an icon, pray to the holy John." John's gospel is one great transfiguration story, already showing us the earthly Jesus in the light of his resurrection. Similarly, icons do not reproduce and portray reality as we see it. With their symbolic forms and colours they symbolize a transfigured reality. An old manual for icon painting states that painters of icons become true iconographers only when they succeed in painting the icon of tranfiguration, when they have learned to paint not with colours but with light.

Because of the special technique used in painting them, the light in icons does not reflect an outside source as in Western art. It comes from within, from the layer of gold and alabaster which shines through the colouring layers of partly transparent yolk colours. This is enhanced through the "inversed perspective". In ancient Greek and Renaissance art, everything is looked at from the point of view of the artist and the onlookers. Subjects in the foreground are thus portrayed larger than those in the background, which creates the impression of three-dimensional space in which everything is enclosed in earthly reality. Icons are painted two-dimensionally, because for the iconographer transcendence is the third dimension. The scenes and persons represented are seen from the perspective of God, above and behind the icon. The bodies therefore appear elongated, and people in the background are often larger than those in the foreground.

As one looks at an icon in meditation, this light coming from within and inversed perspective gradually create an inversion of roles: the observer is taken into the transfigured world and is looked at from a transcendent reality.

Suggestions for Biblical Meditation

Learning from the *lectio divina*

Recently, an adapted form of *lectio divina* has begun to be used for biblical meditation with large groups of young people. Each year the "School of the Word", begun in Milan in 1980 and now spreading to other cities and countries, conducts a series of evenings for all who want to join this meditation within a liturgical framework, often in large cathedrals. Participants receive a printed booklet with Psalms to be recited, biblical texts to be meditated upon, prayers and sung responses. At the beginning the Bible is solemnly brought to the lectern and a Psalm is recited. The biblical passage for the evening is read publicly several times and then reread in silence by the participants. A short explanatory comment follows, in which the leader simply underlines the main affirmations of the text. This leads into a fairly long period of silence, during which each participant works individually on three questions: What does the text say? What does it say to me? How do I respond to the word of God which I hear in this text? A period of prayer and sung responses to God's word follows. The evening ends with participants jotting down in their notebooks any commitments they have made and exchanging with their neighbours what they have learned and how they envisage possible action.

This simple method of corporate biblical meditation, which the "School of the Word" does in large assemblies, can also be used for small group meditation.

Meditating through fantasy journeys

A good text for study by this method is the calling of Levi in Mark 2:13-17. The group reads the passage and makes a list of people and localities mentioned in the text. The enabler then gives some information about the Roman tax and customs system in Palestine, underscoring the ostracized social status of Jews who acted as customs officers. The religious authorities considered them ritually unclean because of their daily contact with non-Jewish money and people. Jewish nationalists despised them as collaborators with the Roman occupying power. Most other people hated them as oppressors who taxed goods at a higher rate than the law prescribed in order to make quick profit.

When the participants in this imaginary journey have reached Capernaum, the animator describes the initial stage of the story as follows: Levi eats alone in his house. As he walks to the customs office at the seashore, where the road leaves Capernaum, people move out of his way. Even children do not greet him. From the point at which Levi reaches the customs office, the story is then told as reported by Mark.

Similar meditations by fantasy journey can be done on Ezekiel's vision of the dry bones (Ezek. 37:1-14), the transfiguration story (Mark 9:2-13) or one of the gospel versions of Jesus' resurrection.

Understanding the Bible with the body

Those who have ever helped to conceive a mime on a biblical text and then participated in enacting it will not soon forget that passage. Somehow it will have entered into their bodies. Here are three examples of possible group mimes:

Make an initial textual study of the parable of the vine and the branches (John 15:1-8). Then ask five persons to mime the text, as the other members help them to find the right postures and movements. One person, representing the vine, stands crouched in the centre, holding by hand on each side someone who is also linked with the two persons on the outside. These four "branches" are deeply bowed down in the form of buds. As the vine grows towards an upright posture, the buds also gradually develop into branches. Then suddenly the link between the left hand of the vine and the two branches on that side is broken. (This should *not* be done by having an additional person portray the vinegrower and cut off the branches — such an addition would divert attention from the main movement of the mime.) The two branches to the left gradually weaken, fade and die while the branches to the right bear rich fruit.

Psalm 8 is first read dramatically, verses 1-2 and 9 by the whole group, verses 3-8 by an individual. Then the group tries to find the right body posture of those who adore and the right body movements of the individual worshipper. Do not try to use movements to portray the babes, animals and birds, for that would detract from the main movement and could easily become ridiculous. The group in adoration stands in a semi-circle, with arms and eyes lifted up to heaven at the beginning and the end and during verses 3-8 following the movements of the individual worshipper with a simple and coordinated gesture of their arms and eyes. This worshipper comes out of the semi-circle to its focal point, still in the posture of adoration (v.3). Then that person falls down into the posture of a foetus (v.4). The difficult part will be the transformation that portrays being lifted up, which must be neither a gradual growth nor an arrogant becoming strong. One must almost see God's hands holding the worshipper under the armpits, lifting the person up and putting him or her on the feet. With gestures of stewardship over creation the worshipper returns into the semi-circle and joins the others in the final posture of adoration.

Attempt with a group to mime Romans 12:2. Which gestures and movements could best express conformity to this age and this world? Which gestures and movements express the renewal of our mind and the discernment of God's will? How can transformation (in the original Greek the term *metamorphōsis* is used) be experienced and shown through our bodies?

Walking with the words of God

The advice we quoted earlier from Martin Luther is essential not only for ministers of the church but for all baptized Christians. As St Anthony said, all of us should be like camels rather than horses. Those who know some Hebrew and Greek would do well to ruminate on short biblical verses in these original languages, because often the original text carries with it shades of meaning which are not conveyed in Bible translations. Any short biblical passage will lend itself well to this type of meditation — sayings of the prophets and of Jesus, short statements of faith from the apostolic letters, verses of the Psalms.

During a Pentecost retreat, a Bible study was first made on the role of the Holy Spirit in John's gospel. Then all the Paraclete passages (John 14:15-18, 14:25-26, 15:26-27, 16:7-11, 16:12-14) were meditated upon through rumination during individual walks. This led in the closing session to a rich sharing of insights.

A revealing text for rumination is Ephesians 2:10, especially if participants have first been taught about the various shades of meaning in the original Greek text: we are God's *poiēma*, God's handiwork, poem, creation. All of us are originals, not just copies. We have been created, re-created in Christ Jesus, and not simply for ourselves, but for good works. These are not *our* good works (cf. Eph. 2:8f.), but the ones which God has already envisaged and prepared for us. In this type of good works we are to walk, step by step. Let a group learn this verse by heart, arrange its wording in such a rhythmic way that one can easily walk with it. Then let the members walk and ruminate for thirty minutes. After reassembling this leads to a sharing of insights about the human life and vocation.

Meditating with icons

Only a very few groups will have access to several good icons. The next best thing is to show a series of slides or reproductions of the great icons.

First show the icon of transfiguration. After a moment of silence, explain to the group some of the characteristics of icon painting. Then show the icons of nativity, crucifixion, the empty tomb and descent to the realm of the dead, concluding with the icon of Pentecost. This must be done mainly in silence, possibly with short appropriate readings from the gospel of John.

Alternatively, only one icon — for example, that of Pentecost or of the Trinity — is shown with short explanations, appropriate readings from the Bible and much silence in between.

During such meditations it may happen that the mysterious reversal of roles of which we spoke earlier takes place: as we look at the icons, the Christ portrayed here begins to look at us and to address us.